YOUR PASSPORT TO

IRAN

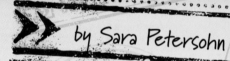

by Sara Petersohn

CONTENT CONSULTANT

Ahoo Najafian, PhD

Postdoctoral Scholar in Middle East Studies

Carleton College

CAPSTONE PRESS

a capstone imprint

Capstone Captivate is published by Capstone Press, an imprint of Capstone.
1710 Roe Crest Drive
North Mankato, Minnesota 56003
www.capstonepub.com

Library of Congress Cataloging-in-Publication Data
Names: Petersohn, Sara, 1959- author.
Title: Your passport to Iran / Sara Petersohn.
Description: North Mankato, Minnesota : Capstone Press, 2021. | Series: World passport | Includes index. | Audience: Grades 4-6
Identifiers: LCCN 2020001013 (print) | LCCN 2020001014 (ebook) | ISBN 9781496684066 (hardcover) | ISBN 9781496687982 (paperback) | ISBN 9781496684578 (pdf)
Subjects: LCSH: Iran--Juvenile literature. | Iran--Social life and customs--Juvenile literature.
Classification: LCC DS254.75 .P48 2021 (print) | LCC DS254.75 (ebook) | DDC 955--dc23
LC record available at https://lccn.loc.gov/2020001013
LC ebook record available at https://lccn.loc.gov/2020001014

Image Credits
AP Images: Alexander Vilf, 27, Ebrahim Noroozi, 25; iStockphoto: BornaMir, 9, efesenko, cover (bottom), geckophotos, 23; Red Line Editorial: 5; Shutterstock Images: Anton_Ivanov, 17, Artography, 6, dowraik, 28, dreibirnen, cover (country), Jakob Fischer, 20, lkpro, 13, Marcin Szymczak, 15, Minda photos, 19, Uskarp, 16, Vladimir Sviracevic, cover (flag)
Design Elements: iStockphoto, Shutterstock Images

Editorial Credits
Editor: Jamie Hudalla; Designer: Colleen McLaren

Printed in the United States of America.
PA117

CONTENTS

Words in **bold** are in the glossary.

CHAPTER ONE

WELCOME TO IRAN!

Tall pillars and stone carvings mark the place where a city once stood. These are the **ruins** of Persepolis in southern Iran. Persian kings built the city in the 500s **BCE**. Parts burned down in 330 BCE. Today, thousands of people from all over the world come to see its ruins. Visitors also discover historical mosques and palaces.

PERSIAN WORDS

Persian and English are related languages. They both belong to the Indo-European language family. Many Persian words sound a lot like English words. The word pronounced *mah-dar* in Persian means "mother" in English. The word pronounced *shesh* means "six." But Persian is written differently from English. It uses an Arabic alphabet. Persian is written from right to left. English is written from left to right.

MAP OF IRAN

Rudkhan Castle

Elburz
Mountains

Marivan

Ali Sadr Cave

■ TEHRAN

IRAN

● Kashan

Naqsh-e
Jahan Square

Dasht-e
Lût Desert

◆ Pasargadae
◆ Persepolis

■ Capital City
● City
⬡ Landform
▲ Landmark
◆ Attraction

N
W E
S

Explore Iran's cities
and landmarks.

People fish in the Caspian
Sea off the coast of Iran.

Iran is a country in the Middle East. More than
84 million people live there. It borders seven other
Middle Eastern countries. These include Iraq and
Afghanistan. Iran's official language is Persian. People
also speak Arabic, Azeri, and several other languages.

FACT FILE

OFFICIAL NAME: ....ISLAMIC REPUBLIC OF IRAN
POPULATION: 84,923,314
LAND AREA: ....591,352 SQ. MI. (1,531,595 SQ KM)
CAPITAL: ....TEHRAN
MONEY: ....RIAL
GOVERNMENT: ....THEOCRATIC REPUBLIC
LANGUAGE: ....PERSIAN
GEOGRAPHY: Located in the Middle East, Iran shares borders with Afghanistan, Armenia, Azerbaijan, Iraq, Pakistan, Turkey, and Turkmenistan.
NATURAL RESOURCES: Iran has oil, natural gas, coal, and metals such as copper and lead.

IRAN'S LANDSCAPE

Iran has many landscapes. The climate is mostly dry. There are deserts in the central and eastern parts of the country. Mountains rise in the north and west. There are olive groves in the north. The southern coast spreads along the Persian Gulf and the Gulf of Oman. The Caspian Sea borders the northern coast.

CHAPTER TWO

HISTORY OF IRAN

Around 1000 BCE, people from central Asia moved west. They came to the region that is now Iran. They became known as the Persians. Cyrus the Great became their king in the 500s BCE. He took control of nearby countries. Later, Persian kings conquered even more lands. The Persian Empire grew. It became one of the biggest ever. It stretched from Greece to India. That's as far as California to Maine!

Alexander the Great of Greece invaded Persia in the 330s BCE. He took control of the area. After he died, the Persian Empire was split up into four parts. One of the parts became the country that is now Iran. But Iran did not get its name until 1935.

OTHER INVADERS

Iran had many rulers over the next 2,000 years. Arabs from Arabia invaded in the 600s **CE**. They brought with them the religion of Islam.

People can visit the tomb of Cyrus the Great in Pasargadae.

More invasions followed. Mongols invaded in the 1200s. Afghans invaded in the 1700s.

By the 1900s, many Iranians felt that the shah, or king, had too much power. Iranians rebelled. They formed a democracy in 1906. But the new government did not last. The next shah took power away from the people. Shahs continued to rule Iran for more than 70 years. Foreign countries also influenced the government. Great Britain and Russia were two of those countries.

INVENTIONS

Iran's climate is mostly hot and dry. Fresh water can be hard to find. Long before electricity, the people of Iran found ways to make life easier. They built a wind tower that catches breezes on top of a house. It sends the wind down into the house. This cools the air inside. They also invented a *qanat*. It uses tunnels to move underground water from the mountains to places with no water. Another cool creation was the ice house. This provides ice all year for desert cities. It has thick mud walls. A pool of water freezes there in winter. It stays frozen in summer.

A REPUBLIC FORMS

In 1979, Iran had another **revolution**. The shah realized he had lost control. He fled the country. A religious leader named Ayatollah Khomeini took charge. He became the Supreme Leader. The country was renamed the Islamic Republic of Iran. The new government included a **constitution**. It had elected officials. But the Supreme Leader had the most power. Iran is now a **theocratic** republic. This means that religious leaders run the government.

TIMELINE OF IRANIAN HISTORY

1000 BCE: The first Persians settle in Iran.

500s BCE: The Persian Empire is established.

330s BCE: Alexander the Great defeats the Persian Empire.

600s CE: Arabs invade and bring the religion of Islam.

1979: The Islamic Republic of Iran forms after a revolution.

1989: Ali Khamenei becomes Supreme Leader of Iran.

2013: Hassan Rouhani becomes president.

2015: Countries including the United States make an agreement with Iran to limit Iran's **nuclear** weapons activity.

2018: The United States backs out of the nuclear agreement.

AFTER THE REVOLUTION

In 1980, Iraq invaded Iran. The war cost many lives. It ended in 1988. Both sides agreed to stop fighting. Starting in the 1970s, tensions grew between Iran and the United States. Some Iranian citizens took more than 50 Americans hostage. The hostages were held for more than a year. In 2013, Hassan Rouhani became president. He and U.S. President Barack Obama spoke by phone. The leaders hoped to end conflict between the countries.

CHAPTER THREE

EXPLORE IRAN

Iran has many ancient sites. Naqsh-e Rostam is a large cemetery. It has the tombs of four Persian kings. Ancient artwork is carved on the rocks outside these tombs.

People visit the city of Esfahan. They go to Naqsh-e Jahan Square. This large square was built in the 1600s. It has the Sheikh Lotfollah Mosque and Shah Mosque. They are beautiful examples of Persian art and **architecture**. Soon after the square was built, Iran's fifth shah ordered a six-story palace to be built there. The palace gave the shah a great view of the **polo** matches played in the square. Today, there is a huge pool where the polo field used to be. Children swim and cool off in this pool in the summer.

Naqsh-e Jahan Square has a large mosque and reflecting pool.

Iranians enjoy shopping at bazaars. Bazaars are markets. The Grand Bazaar in Tehran has more than 6 miles (9.7 kilometers) of alleys. Merchants sell carpets, spices, and other goods. The Iran Mall is also in Tehran. It became the largest shopping mall in the world when it opened in 2018. It has more than 700 shops, 200 restaurants, 15 sports fields, and 12 theaters!

MOUNTAINS AND DESERTS

Many people visit Iran's mountains. People ski there in winter. They hike in summer. Wolves, bears, leopards, eagles, and other animals live in the mountains. Storks **migrate** to the city of Marivan. People there build nests for the birds. Storks are a symbol of blessing in Iran.

Green forests grow on the northern slopes of the Elburz Mountains. Visitors hike up the mountains. They can see the Caspian Sea.

The Dasht-e Lūt desert is one
of the hottest places in the world.

Two large deserts spread across the middle of Iran.
A crust of salt covers the Dasht-e Kavir desert. The
Dasht-e Lūt is a sand desert. Almost nothing lives
in these deserts. Their harsh climate makes them
dangerous places to visit. Dasht-e Lūt's temperature
once reached 159 degrees Fahrenheit (71 degrees
Celsius). It is one of the hottest places on Earth!

Rudkhan Castle was built more than 1,000 years ago.

Ali Sadr Cave is a water cave.

CASTLES AND CAVES

Travelers enjoy visiting many old castles. Ancient Persians built Rudkhan Castle high on a mountain. This protected it from Arab invaders. More than 1,000 years later, visitors can still see its towers, jail, and king's rooms. Caves also attract visitors. Ali Sadr Cave is more than 6.8 miles (11 km) long. Deep water covers its floor. People explore this cave by boat.

FACT

Iran is the last remaining home of the Asiatic cheetah. There may be fewer than 200 of these large cats still alive.

CHAPTER FOUR

DAILY LIFE

Iranians value education. More than 85 percent of those who are 15 or older can read and write. Children must attend school from ages 6 to 11. Most attend longer. Boys and girls go to separate schools. Many go to college. All students are required to study the Qur'an. This is Islam's holy book.

FACT

By law, people dress modestly in Iran. From the age of nine, girls must cover their heads and necks when they are in public. They usually wear a head scarf or a **chador**. Boys wear long pants.

Students go to school from Saturday through Thursday. Families often visit friends and relatives in the evening. On weekends, young people go to coffee shops, restaurants, and cultural events.

Some schools in Iran take field trips to Naqsh-e Jahan Square.

Many people in Iran like to drink tea.

FACT

Nomads have roamed the mountains and deserts of Iran since ancient times. They move from place to place to find grass for their animals. These nomads come from many ethnic groups. They include Turks, Persians, Kurds, and Arabs. Today, the nomadic lifestyle is disappearing. More and more nomadic people settle in cities and find jobs there.

FOOD AND HOSPITALITY

A simple breakfast in Iran might include cheese, bread, jam, and tea. Most meals are served with rice, grilled meat, and vegetables. Bread, yogurt, and fruit are common too.

Iranians love to invite people into their homes. They offer guests hot tea and often sweet treats to go with it. Tea is a favorite drink in Iran. Coffee shops that sell herbal teas are popular. Friends often gather at these places.

PERSIAN WALNUT COOKIES

These cookies are a traditional treat during Nowruz. This is the Persian New Year celebration. With the help of an adult, you can bake these cookies at home.

Cookie Ingredients:
- 3 egg yolks
- ½ cup sugar
- 1 ½ cups of chopped walnuts
- 2 tablespoons chopped pistachio nuts

Cookie Directions:

1. Preheat the oven to 300°F.
2. In a bowl, mix together the egg yolks and sugar.
3. Add the chopped walnuts and mix well.
4. Line a cookie sheet with parchment paper. Using a teaspoon, drop heaping scoops of cookie dough onto the parchment paper. Leave a few inches between cookies.
5. Sprinkle a little bit of the chopped pistachio nuts on top of each cookie.
6. Bake the cookies for 35 to 45 minutes. Remove the pan from the oven and place cookies on a cooling rack. Then move the cookies onto a plate.

CHAPTER FIVE

HOLIDAYS AND CELEBRATIONS

The most festive holiday in Iran is the Persian New Year. It is called Nowruz. It begins on the first day of spring. Nowruz represents new beginnings. People clean their homes to prepare for Nowruz. They make special meals. They buy new clothes. Most importantly, they set up the Haft Sin table. The table includes at least seven items. The items have names beginning with the letter *S* in Persian. The table might have wheat sprouts, apples, garlic, vinegar, sumac, silver berry, and sweet pudding. Other items could be the Qur'an, mirrors, candles, and colored eggs. Sometimes a book of poetry by the Persian poet Hafez is included. On the last Tuesday night before Nowruz, people build small bonfires in the streets.

People prepare special meals for Nowruz.

The celebration lasts 13 days. Families often gather or travel together during this time. The 13th day is Sizdah Bedar. On this day, families eat picnic lunches outside. They throw the sprouts from the Haft Sin table into rivers. This marks the end of the Nowruz celebration. It is the start of a new year.

RELIGIOUS HOLIDAYS

Religious holidays are important in Iran. Islam is the state religion. People who belong to Islam are called Muslims. More than 99 percent of people in Iran are Muslims. Ramadan is a holy month for them. It is the ninth month of the Muslim calendar. This calendar is based on the cycles of the moon. Muslims pray together in mosques during Ramadan. They do not eat or drink from dawn until dusk every day. They eat meals after sunset and before sunrise.

The last day of Ramadan is call Eid al-Fitr. This is a major holiday. Muslims celebrate with a feast.

Muslims pray together during Eid al-Fitr.

CHAPTER SIX

SPORTS AND RECREATION

Iranians love the sport of wrestling. Iran has earned more than 40 Olympic medals in wrestling. They have also done well at weight lifting.

Wrestling is thought of as Iran's national sport. But soccer is the country's most popular sport. It is called football in Iran. Children often play soccer in the streets. Iran's men's soccer team has won three Asian Cups. They haven't won the World Cup yet. But they have qualified for it five times.

FACT

In 2012, weight lifter Behdad Salimikordasiabi lifted more than 500 pounds (220 kilograms) over his head. He won an Olympic gold medal.

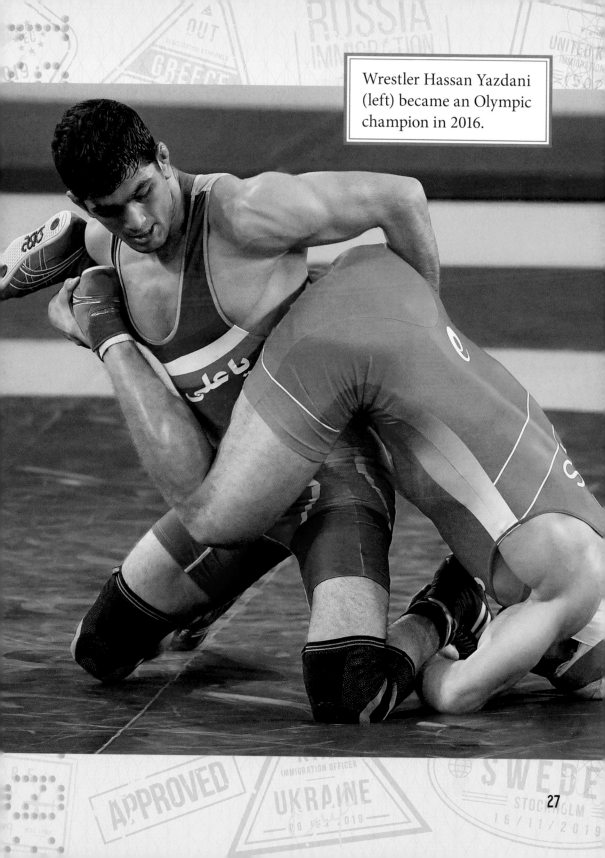

Wrestler Hassan Yazdani (left) became an Olympic champion in 2016.

Tourists can go on camel rides in Kashan, Iran.

OUTDOOR AND INDOOR ACTIVITIES

There are many mountain activities in Iran. These include snow sports in winter and hiking in summer. People enjoy sandboarding in the desert. They ride snowboards down the dunes. People also bike in the desert. Camel rides are popular too.

A favorite board game in Iran is backgammon. The game has been played for thousands of years. In Iran, it is often played in parks and tea houses.

Iran is full of amazing sites. There are huge shopping centers and beautiful places of worship. Iran has many incredible places to visit.

KABADDI

Kabaddi is a popular game of tag in Iran. It is played with two teams. Official games require 12 players on each team. Unofficially, it can be played with as few as three players per team.

1. Each team uses half the playing area as its territory.
2. Someone called a raider runs onto the other team's territory. The raider tags as many of the other team's players as possible, while shouting "Kabaddi! Kabaddi! Kabaddi!" repeatedly without taking a breath.
3. The raider runs back to his or her own side. Everyone the raider tags is out. Then a raider from the other team goes.
4. If the other team tackles the raider, or the raider doesn't make it back to the team's territory before running out of breath, the raider is out.
5. A team scores a point when someone on the opposite team is tagged.

GLOSSARY

architecture (AR-kuh-tek-chuhr) the style of buildings

BCE/CE BCE means Before Common Era, or before year one. CE means Common Era, or after year one

chador (CHA-dor) a long, dark, loose cloak that is worn by some women in Iran to cover their heads and bodies

constitution (kon-stuh-TOO-shun) the system of laws that state the rights of the people and the powers of the government

migrate (MYE-grate) to move from one area to another

nomads (NO-mads) people who roam from place to place, not settling in one location

nuclear (NOO-klee-ur) having to do with a reaction that releases a dangerous form of energy

polo (POH-loh) a game played on horseback using wooden mallets and balls

revolution (rev-uh-LOO-shun) the overthrow of a government, replacing it with a new government

ruins (ROO-ins) the remains of an ancient structure

theocratic (thee-uh-KRAH-tik) having to do with a form of government run by religious leaders

READ MORE

Mattern, Joanne. *Iran*. Buffalo, NY: Cavendish Square, 2018.

Murray, Julie. *Iran*. Minneapolis, MN: Abdo, 2016.

Sovereign, Danielle. *Explore Iran: 12 Key Facts*. Mankato, MN: 12-Story Library, 2019.

INTERNET SITES

DK Find Out!: Caspian Sea
https://www.dkfindout.com/us/earth/oceans-and-seas/caspian-sea

National Geographic Kids: Celebrating Ramadan
https://kids.nationalgeographic.com/explore/history/ramadan

National Geographic Kids: Iran
https://kids.nationalgeographic.com/explore/countries/iran

INDEX

OTHER BOOKS IN THIS SERIES

YOUR PASSPORT TO CHINA

YOUR PASSPORT TO ECUADOR

YOUR PASSPORT TO EL SALVADOR

YOUR PASSPORT TO ETHIOPIA

YOUR PASSPORT TO FRANCE

YOUR PASSPORT TO KENYA

YOUR PASSPORT TO PERU

YOUR PASSPORT TO RUSSIA

YOUR PASSPORT TO SPAIN